Archaeology
and the
Enigma of Fort Raleigh

Archaeology and the Enigma of Fort Raleigh

by
J. C. Harrington

Raleigh
America's Four Hundredth Anniversary Committee
North Carolina Department of Cultural Resources
1984

America's Four Hundredth Anniversary Committee

Lindsay C. Warren, Jr.
Chairman

Marc Basnight	William S. Powell	Mrs. Margo Tillett
Andy Griffith	L. Richardson Preyer	Charles B. Wade, Jr.
John P. Kennedy	David Stick	John F. Wilson IV
Robert V. Owens, Jr.	James A. Summers	Charles B. Winberry, Jr.
	Mrs. J. Emmet Winslow	

John D. Neville
Executive Director

Mrs. Marsden B. deRosset, Jr.
Assistant Director

Advisory Committee on Publications

William S. Powell
Chairman

Lindley S. Butler
Jerry C. Cashion
David Stick
Alan D. Watson

ISBN 0-86526-203-9

Contents

Illustrations

Foreword

America's Four Hundredth Anniversary Committee, formed in 1978 under the provisions of an act of the North Carolina General Assembly of 1973, was charged with recommending plans for the observance of the quadricentennial of the first English attempts to explore and settle North America. The committee has proposed to carry out a variety of programs to appeal to a broad range of people. Among these is a publications program that includes a series of booklets dealing with the history of the events and people of the 1580s.

Queen Elizabeth I of England enjoyed a reign that was for the most part peaceful. It was a period of prosperity, which saw the flourishing of a new interest in literature, religion, exploration, and business. English mariners began to venture farther from home, and in time talk began to be heard of hopes to establish naval bases and colonies in America. Men of the County of Devon in the southwest of England, seafarers for generations, played leading roles in this expansion. One of these, Walter Ralegh (as he most often wrote his name), became a favorite of the queen, and on him she bestowed a variety of honors and rewards. It was he to whom she granted a charter in 1584 authorizing the discovery and occupation of lands not already held by "any Christian Prince and . . . people." Ralegh promptly sent a reconnaissance expedition to what is now North Carolina, and this was followed in due time by a colony under the leadership of Ralph Lane. Headquarters were established on Roanoke Island. After remaining for nearly a year and exploring far afield, Lane and his men returned to England in 1586.

In the summer of 1587 Governor John White and a colony of 115 men, women, and children arrived and occupied the houses and the fort left by Lane. The brief annals of this colony are recorded in a journal kept by the governor; they tell of certain problems that arose early—but they also record the birth of the first English child in America. The journal further explains why Governor White consented to return to England for supplies. His departure was the last contact with the settlers who constituted the "Lost Colony," renowned in history, literature, and folklore.

Although a casual acquaintance with the facts of these English efforts might suggest that they were failures, such was far from the case. Ralegh's expenditures of time, effort, and resources (in which he was joined by many others, including Queen Elizabeth herself) had salutary effects for England and certainly for all of present-day America. From Ralegh's initial investment in the reconnaissance voyage, as well as from the colonies, came careful descriptions of the New World and samples of its products. The people of England, indeed of the Western world, learned about North America; because books were published based on what Ralegh's men discovered, they could soon read for themselves of the natives there and the promise of strange and wonderful new resources.

From these voyages and colonizing efforts came the conviction that an English nation could be established in America. In 1606, when another charter was about to be issued for further settlement, King James, who succeeded Queen Elizabeth at her death in 1603, called for advice from some of the men who had been associated with Ralegh. They assured the king that further efforts would surely succeed. With this the Virginia Company was chartered, and it established England's first permanent settlement in America at Jamestown.

Because of Sir Walter Ralegh's vision, England persisted. Because of England's persistence and its refusal to yield to Spain's claims to the region, the United States today enjoys an English heritage. The English common law is the basis of American law; American legislative bodies are modeled on the House of Commons with the rights and freedoms that it developed over a long period of time; America's mother tongue is English, and it is the most commonly spoken language in the world—pilots and navigators on international airlines and the controllers who direct them at airports all over the world use English. Americans also share England's literary tradition: Chaucer, Beowulf, King Arthur, and Shakespeare are America's too, and Americans can enjoy Dickens and Tennyson, as well as Agatha Christie and Dorothy Sayers. America's religious freedom is also in the English tradition, and several of this nation's Protestant denominations trace their earliest history to origins in England: the Episcopal church, certainly, but the Quakers, Baptists, Congregationalists, and Universalists as well.

America's Four Hundredth Anniversary Committee has planned many programs to direct national and even international attention to the significance of events that occurred from bases established by English men, women, and children, but notably Sir Walter Ralegh, in what is now North Carolina during the period 1584-1590. While some of the programs may be regarded as fleeting and soon forgotten, the publications are intended to serve as lasting reminders of America's indebtedness to England. Books and pamphlets covering a broad range of topics have been prepared by authors on both sides of the Atlantic. These, it is anticipated, will introduce a vast new audience to the facts of America's origins.

Lindsay C. Warren, Jr., *Chairman*
America's Four Hundredth Anniversary Committee

I. An Archaeological Challenge

A very definite air of mystery has always surrounded Fort Raleigh. Intensive research, both documentary and archaeological, has done nothing to diminish this special quality. In fact, it has only added to the enigma of the site speculation concerning the exact location of the settlement. Hidden away in a wooded section of Roanoke Island on the Outer Banks of North Carolina, the earthen structure, assumed to be what was left of a fort built in 1585 by the first English colonists in the Western Hemisphere, was for years little known and seldom visited. Governor Ralph Lane, who directed the construction of the fort, called it simply "the new fort in Virginia," but in more recent times the ruins of the structure, as well as the presumed settlement site, have come to be called Fort Raleigh. (This term was probably used for the first time in the deed to a 10-acre parcel of land sold in 1894 to the newly formed Roanoke Colony Memorial Association, an organization formed for the purpose of preserving the traditional fort site.)

The study and restudy of numerous contemporary documents having relevance to the Roanoke Island colonizing ventures did little to solve the enigma of Fort Raleigh, so the science of archaeology was called upon to attempt to provide the answers. This publication will describe how archaeological research has been employed at the site and what new evidence has come from this research. In many ways, archaeological research has only added to the mysteries of Fort Raleigh, but it has produced some quite unexpected results and has enabled the area to be more effectively interpreted to visitors. The site fully merits the designation as one of the nation's most significant historic places.

Two important occurrences in relatively recent years have had a lasting effect, not only upon the site iself but also upon the widespread perception by the public of Fort Raleigh's place in American history. First was the inauguration of Paul Green's *The Lost Colony*, an outdoor drama presented on the shore of Roanoke Island only a short distance from the fort, where it has been produced every summer since 1937 (except during World War II). *The Lost Colony* has provided an insight into the historic events surrounding this significant episode in American history and into the way English colonists lived and died 400 years ago. It has added a more sophisticated and credible interpretation of the Raleigh colonizing ventures. More important, it has helped focus public interest on an obscure relic of outstanding national significance. The second event occurred in 1940 with the transfer of the historic site to the National Park Service, United States Department of the Interior, and its designation the following year as Fort Raleigh National Historic Site. Eventually the site tract was increased to 144 acres in order to encompass the probable settlement area and to provide room for administrative and public-use facilities without the danger of encroachment on historic remains.

The National Park Service immediately realized that more needed to be known about the site before it could be adequately interpreted to the visiting public, especially since *The Lost Colony* was presented only during the summer—and then only in the evening. The situation clearly called for archaeological investigation—not merely as a last resort, but to round out the story suggested by the historical records. World War II began before any excavating could be undertaken, although the Park Service initiated a program of documentary research even before it acquired the site; this research began with the pioneering work of Charles W. Porter III, chief of the Planning and Interpretation Section, Historic Sites Branch, National Park Service. Various historians have continued this phase of the research, sometimes with conflicting interpretations, right through to the recent reexamination of the contemporary documentary evidence by researcher Phillip Evans.[1] Of outstanding importance have been the contributions of David B. Quinn, whose definitive publications[2] are basic to any research involving the colonies on Roanoke Island.

Documentary evidence concerning a historic site is nearly always fragmentary and frequently ambiguous. Fortunately, the missing evidence is often the very kind that might be contributed by archaeology. In addition to filling in some of the gaps in the written record, archaeology can usually be counted on to provide a better interpretation of the documentary evidence as well as to resolve certain ambiguities. At Fort Raleigh, even with an abundant supply of documentary material, the sort of information that throws light on the way these first English settlers lived—their everyday life—is, on the whole, missing. But most important of all, the records fail to explain exactly where the settlement was. An archaeologist, of course, cannot provide the missing ingredients in the historical record until he or she has a site on which to dig. Therefore, one

2

of the first tasks at Fort Raleigh was to ascertain the precise area of settlement.

By 1947 the National Park Service was able to launch a limited archaeological program that lasted off and on through 1953 under the author's supervision in the field. Even in its early state, the excavation at Fort Raleigh attracted considerable attention from archaeologists and historians inasmuch as the excavation of sites of European origin was a new approach to American history and archaeological method. This pioneering example of combined documentary-archaeological research played a major role in developing the new discipline of historical archaeology and helped set the standard for future work in this field.

Archaeologists no longer dig at random in the hope that something important or exciting will be found. Excavation and all the research that goes with it are planned in advance insofar as is feasible. But even before planning an excavation at a historic site, let along starting to dig, it is essential to study all readily available records pertaining to the site and to prepare questions that might be answered by archaeology. Relying upon these questions and innumerable practical considerations such as financing, the threat of damage to the site, and future interpretive development, archaeologists tentatively establish priorities for individual projects and develop an excavating program. Of course, it usually happens that answering one question leads to another not anticipated at the start, and the entire program may have to be altered as the project progresses. At Fort Raleigh, archaeology failed to answer the most important question of all: Where was the settlement located? This obviously disrupted the long-range program, which had anticipated the careful excavation of each of the original building sites.

Well before any excavating was even tentatively planned, thorough research into the documents relating to the colonizing venture was carried out and detailed reports prepared. It was apparent that the site called for two disparate but related projects, each dealing with a separate area and each with its own special problems. One was the known site—the surface remains traditionally accepted as Ralph Lane's "new fort in Virginia." The second—the settlement where the colonists lived—was known only from historical references, and these provided only a very general idea of its location. It seemed logical, therefore, to initiate archaeological fieldwork at the fort site in the hope that this would not only reveal something definite about the particular structure but might also provide some clue as to the location of the habitation area. Moreover, the indistinct contours that marked the fort site—which was all the National Park Service had to show visitors—required more adequate interpretation.

Two questions needed to be answered, if possible, before a more extensive excavation of the fort could be planned. First, were these visible surface traces actually the remains of Lane's fort; or, at the very least, did they date from the time of the settlement? Second, was there likely to be enough evidence left at the site to warrant a full-scale dig? There was justification in asking each of these questions, although they must have seemed pointless to those who held steadfastly to the traditional identification and could see no other valid explanation for the ruins being there.

Both tradition and the study of records relating to the Roanoke Island colonizing venture seemed to leave no doubt that both the fort and the settlement had been built at the north end of the island. But there were minor ambiguities in the record that raised questions about the site's precise location. Before the National Park Service became responsible for the site, the agency felt that the authenticity of the site should be established once and for all before major excavating and site development were carried out. It was felt that a minor test excavation might erase any remaining uncertainty; at least it was worth a try.

Along an entirely different line, there was good reason to wonder whether the extensive activity at the site over the years might have played havoc with any relevant archaeological remains. It seemed to have been the fate of this site that everything imaginable happened to it (although it is remarkable what archaeologists can do with very little evidence).

It is recorded that soldiers stationed on Roanoke Island during the Civil War dug into the ruins. The amount of damage done by them is not known, but it was probably very little. Even before this, visitors to the site undoubtedly had removed many, if not all, the objects still visible on the ground, although there is no historical evidence that they did any digging. John Lawson, a historian and traveler from England, for example, found, and presumably carried away, "a Brass-Gun, a Powder Horn, and one small Quarter-deck-Gun" during a visit to Roanoke Island around 1700.[3] And, of course, there were the local Indians, who were in the area for some time after the colonists left and who must have salvaged every visible artifact that appealed to them.

Fortunately, little interest could be elicited for the three hundredth anniversary in 1885, probably sparing the site additional damage. Nevertheless, an amateur archaeologist, Talcott Williams, visited the area in 1887. Williams was primarily concerned with Indian sites on

Roanoke Island, but, as did many others in later years, he became intrigued by the fort remains and did considerable digging at the site in 1895. The only thing at all commendable about this affair is that Williams wrote and published a fairly good report in which he described the thirteen trenches he dug at the fort.

By that time, Fort Raleigh was coming into its own. In 1896 the newly formed Roanoke Colony Memorial Association erected an impressive stone monument commemorating the birth of Virginia Dare, the first English child to be born in the colony. The placement of this large stone on an even larger brick base squarely in the estimated center of the fort did some damage in this important location—but not nearly so much as was done some thirty years later, when the monument and base were removed. The Memorial Association also put some small stone markers along what appeared to be the crest of the still-visible ridges of the fort, although the markers actually did very little damage to the ruins.

Fortunately, after this first effort to mark the fort for commemoration, the site was left alone for several years; and it was not until 1921 that the custodians of the tract committed another minor indiscretion by allowing a motion picture to be filmed there. This undertaking involved digging a deep trench along one side of the ruins, an intrusion that stood out prominently when the fort was fully excavated in 1950. It is doubtful that the trench enhanced the movie sufficiently to justify the damage done to the site. Obviously, the idea of preserving buried historic remains had not yet been seriously considered. Nor had the notion been entertained by 1936, when, as part of a public works project, several incongruous log structures were erected over the presumed settlement area and the fort was "restored." The restoration consisted of the addition of a stockade of heavy logs, sunk in a deep trench, that conformed approximately to the outline of the fort ruins. But worse still, a log blockhouse was built on a stone footing at the very center of the fort—a final impediment, it was feared, to finding any helpful archaeological evidence in the area that otherwise could be expected to be the most productive. No wonder there was some doubt as to whether enough of the fort remained to make a full-scale excavation worthwhile! Nevertheless, historians were unhappy with the 1936 reconstruction, and scholarly discipline (as well as just plain curiosity) virtually compelled the National Park Service to consider serious archaeological exploration of the fort ruins. The two main problems were to "sell" this kind of archaeology and to "un-sell" the idea that Englishmen had built the log cabins in 1585.

II. The Traditional Fort Comes to Life

The first thing an archaeologist does when beginning a new excavation is to establish permanent reference points so that everything uncovered can be accurately recorded, both in plan and elevation and in relation to other features disclosed in the excavating. It was anticipated that at Fort Raleigh such other features might include anything thrown away or intentionally left behind by the colonists and not carried off by the Indians (for example, kitchen refuse, broken and discarded tools and utensils, personal articles, and the like), structural features, pits and other intrusions, and stratified redeposits of earth. All such information is duly recorded in drawings and in notebooks and, when feasible, photographed. An archaeologist must be a competent surveyor, photographer, and draftsman and must have the right touch with trowel and whisk broom. Recording procedures are facilitated by laying out an arbitrary grid system, to which all measurements can be related. A pre-excavation contour map is also advantageous, and such a map was prepared for Fort Raleigh.

Faced with surface remains as indistinct and confusing as those at Fort Raleigh, archaeologists resorted to considerable guesswork in deciding where to dig the first exploratory trenches. One helpful guide was to avoid Talcott Williams's test pits, the approximate location of which were known from his report. (At least Williams reported where he did *not* dig.) During the 1947 season four trenches were dug, each revealing a cross section through the original fort ditch ("dry moat"); this is typical of an earthwork in which earth from a ditch is thrown up to form a parapet. But best of all, two of the trenches disclosed the location of the main fort entrance (the importance of which will be discussed later).

No diagnostic artifacts were found in these first four trenches (or none that were thought to be useful in dating the structure, other than to conclude that it was almost certainly of the settlement period). It was clear, however, that the original structure had been an earthwork that conformed approximately to the low ridges and shallow depressions still visible on the ground. Examination of the fills in the original fort ditches showed that there had been an early, rapid deposit in the bottom

6

few inches, probably soon after the fort was built. Above this initial silt deposit was an accumulation from further erosion of the parapet; the accumulation consisted of earth from a series of rapid fillings interspersed with layers of humus. This is exactly what one would expect to have happened at the site—occasional erosion by abnormally heavy rains interrupted by slow development of typical forest humus. At that point there could be no doubt that the structure was old and must surely meet the age requirements for Ralph Lane's "new fort."

As to the potential for a major exploration of the site, the preliminary archaeological evidence was most reassuring. The trench for the 1936 stockade, although it must have intercepted the fort ditch in places, was probably not going to be as great a hindrance as feared. There was less optimism concerning the interior of the fort, an area estimated to have been roughly 50 feet square; but it was the most critical portion of the fort and would have to be excavated, past disturbance notwithstanding.

Before excavating this important area, however, more needed to be known about the overall plan of the fort—in other words, the ground plan of the entire fort ditch. This information was gathered in 1948 during the second season of the project by digging a series of short trenches at intervals across the calculated position of the ditch—but just deeply enough to distinguish the outline of the ditch fill. Identifying this material was not too difficult, for the darker fill showed up in marked contrast to the adjacent undisturbed tannish clay subsoil as soon as the topsoil had been removed.

There now existed an approximate layout that could be compared with typical plans of small earthworks of the period and with a fort built on the island of Puerto Rico, where Sir Richard Grenville's colonists stopped to gather salt while on their way to Roanoke Island in 1585. John White made a drawing of this structure, which he labeled "The forme of a fort which was made by Master Ralfe Lane . . . where we toke in salt. . . ." Both of the forts attributed to Ralph Lane followed the general plan used at that time for small defensive works—namely, a square with bastions extending outward from three sides. It was just about then that bastions, because of their greater effectiveness against the use of gunfire, began to be placed at the corners of the square by military engineers. Once the plan of Fort Raleigh had been determined and compared with White's drawing, the superficial similarity between the two earthworks became highly encouraging. In the end, however, the dating of Fort Raleigh was dependent upon the age of excavated artifacts and not merely upon Lane's conservative military inclinations.

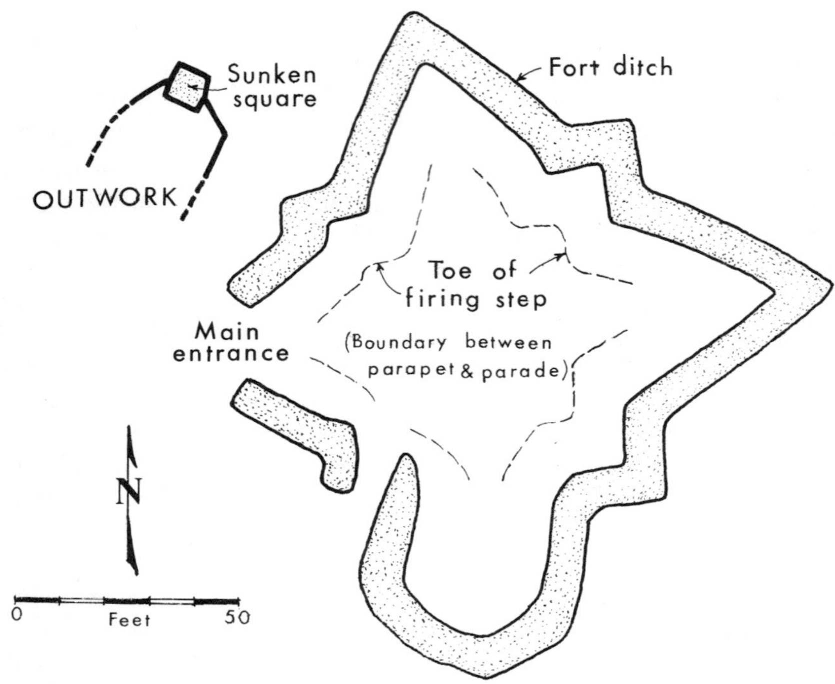

Plan of excavated fort and outwork, showing only those features dating from the sixteenth-century colonizing ventures, as revealed through archaeology. Plan drawn and supplied by the author.

In addition to providing a general plan of the fort ditch, these shallow exploratory trenches showed that there probably had been no "glacis" along the outer edge of the ditch, although this feature is normal for earthen forts.[4]

Following the successful preliminary excavations in 1947 and 1948, a project was set up in 1950 for a meticulous excavation of the entire fort, to be followed, if the evidence warranted, by reconstruction of the earthwork. The first step was to excavate the interior or "parade" of the fort, as well as the area under the original parapet. Afterward, the fort ditch could be completely dug out and the earth thrown up to form the parapet; thus, in a sense, the process used by the original builders would be duplicated.

As expected—and feared—the interior of the fort was utter confusion. Every one of the disturbances described above was found, as were others, which was quite a surprise. The continuous stockade trench from the 1936 reconstruction was discovered to have caused less

8

damage than originally feared, and the 1921 motion picture trench was an annoyance but not calamitous. A small circular disturbance, not otherwise identified, may have been the place where the Civil War soldiers are reputed to have dug. The owner of the land, as the story has been handed down, stopped this depredation at an early stage; or these alleged looters, being typical soldiers, may simply have run out of steam. Far more damaging than any of the recorded activities were two large instrusions—both relatively recent—near the center of the parade. Each of them went down some 3 feet and contained rolls of modern wire fencing. Because one of them cut into a Talcott Williams test hole, they were identified as post-1895 disturbances.[5] These large pits may well have been dug by the inquisitive crew that built the log blockhouse and

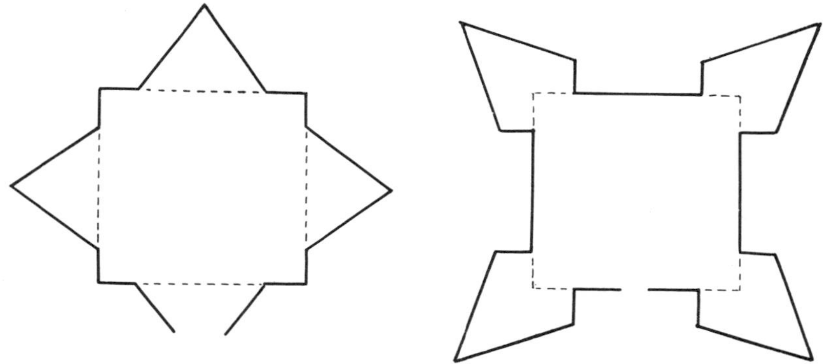

Two quite different plans for small earthworks were in use at the time of the Ralegh settlements. In the older type (left), bastions were placed on the sides of the basic square. This served well when defenders were armed with pikes and halberds. When guns came into greater use, a new scheme, employing bastions at the corners of the square (right), proved more satisfactory. Ralph Lane, obviously, preferred the older type (although his soldiers used both muskets and small cannon), and he employed this version both at Fort Raleigh and at the temporary fort erected in Puerto Rico while he was en route to the new colony. Plan drawn and supplied by the author.

stockade, or they could possibly date from the excavation connected with the 1921 movie. On top of every feature and instrusion were the stone footings of the 1936 blockhouse reconstruction. One might almost think of this as the final effort to confuse some future archaeologist.

Only one feature was found in the area of the parade that predates the numerous disturbances described above: an unrecorded intrusion over 30 feet long and from 7 to 11 feet wide, extending some 12 inches into the subsoil. No artifacts or structural remains were found within it, but its stratigraphic relationship to other datable features suggests that it might have some connection with the original earthwork—possibly the depressed floor of a structure in the center of the fort. It is known from contemporary accounts that there was at least one building in the fort and that it had a thatched roof. Obviously, a fort, however sparsely garrisoned, would have had housing for the soldiers and storage rooms for weapons, ammunition, and provisions.

It was somewhat surprising not to have found evidence of a well, but under the difficult excavating conditions such a feature could easily have been missed. The only way to be sure would have been to dig down below every intrusion, but this did not seem feasible at the time. In addition, the numerous sherds of large Spanish olive jars suggested that water for the men stationed in the fort was kept in these vessels.

Archaeologists depend largely upon artifacts or man-made objects for dating intrusions and soil levels. But not a single artifact was found in any of the features encountered in the parade area—with the sole exception of a brass rifle cartridge in one of Talcott Williams's trenches—although the wire fencing (which technically might be called an artifact) did establish that the two large intrusions were of relatively recent date. A few items of interest were left in this area, but none were in a situation that provides help in dating features or strata. Most intriguing of all were three metal discs, about an inch in diameter, that looked like thin coins. They turned out to be casting counters, used with a counting board (or cloth) for manual reckoning—after the fashion of an abacus. Clearly, they fit into the period of the settlement; but, quite obviously, they were not being used for their original purpose inasmuch as they all had one or two holes punched through them, making them unfit for use with a counting cloth. They were probably brought over by the colonists for the express purpose of trading with the Indians, who would find them extremely attractive as strung ornaments.[6]

One of the important contributions of the 1950 excavation of the parade was that it showed that the ground level at the time the fort was completed was 4 or 5 inches below the surrounding natural level; in other words, the original humus layer had been removed. But since the original topsoil was still in place under the parapet remnants, it is apparent that the interior of the fort was lowered after the parapet was built—possibly to obtain earth to form the firing step (the "banquette") behind the parapet. This discovery was most helpful, for it marked the edge of the firing step, thus providing important information for restoring the above-ground portion of the fort.

10

Excavation of the area covered by the original parapet proved more productive than that of the parade. Averaging about 20 feet in width, this strip had been disturbed less than the interior (except by the 1936 stockade)—probably because the center of any archaeological feature is always the most appealing point to relic hunters, whether it is an Egyptian pyramid or an Indian mound. Most of the earth that had originally been thrown up from the fort ditch and shaped to form the parapet had subsequently eroded back into the adjacent ditch, but some was left—in several places, almost a foot thick. This remnant of the parapet gave some protection to the original ground surface, so any artifacts or features found on the original ground were probably there when the first earth was thrown out to begin construction of the parapet.

Only one man-made feature was found in the protected strip: a small Indian campfire, or hearth. This feature, as well as several sherds of Indian pottery found scattered on the original surface under the parapet, suggests that Indians had been there before 1585. The campfire

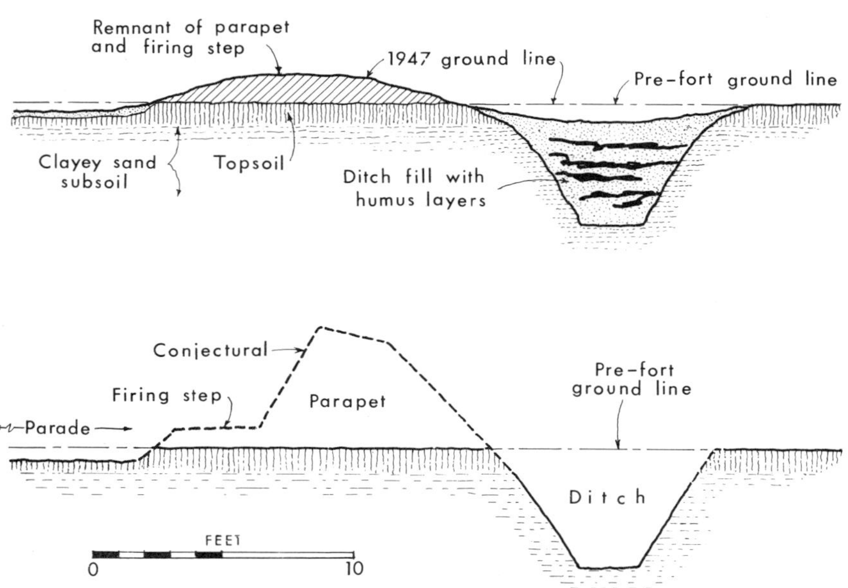

Actual and conjectural sections through fort ditch and parapet. (Top): Evidence uncovered through excavating, showing how most of the parapet had eroded into the ditch and that humus layers had developed in the ditch fill between periods of heavier erosion. (Bottom): Conjectural reconstruction of the ditch, parapet, and firing step. Note that the interior of the fort (the "parade") had been lowered several inches below the original ground line. Plan drawn and supplied by the author.

contained several rough, shalelike stones whose pointed bases presumably were used to support unwieldy cooking pots.

The only other artifacts of any significance found under or in the parapet remnant was a group of eight typical wrought iron spikes with "mushroom" heads, the longest being 7 inches in length. It appeared that some careless workman had dropped a bundle or bag of spikes on the ground at an early stage in the fort's construction and that the spikes were immediately covered with earth thrown out of the ditch and were soon forgotten. Three similar spikes and several iron nails were found within the fort, but not in so revealing a location as the group of eight. One cannot help wondering what such items were doing at the settlement, let alone at the fort, during this early stage in its construction.[7]

3 CM

Front and back of one of three casting counters, about 1 inch in diameter, found at the fort excavation. These thin, stamped discs of a cheap alloy were made in Germany and used in manual reckoning on a ruled table or cloth but were probably brought to the new colony as items of trade with the Indians. With a hole punched in each of them, they would have been quite appealing to the Indians as strung ornaments. From Harrington, *Search for the Cittie of Ralegh*, Figure 17.

Having shown rather convincingly that the traditional fort site did indeed date from the period of the Ralegh settlement, the next question was what to do with it. Policy and precedent militated against reconstructing the structure; but merely marking the fort's outlines on the ground would be an unexciting way to exhibit such an important site to the public. On the other hand, rebuilding the earthwork seemed both feasible and justified. The fort ditch could be restored to almost exactly its original shape. Actually, it would not just be *like* the original ditch—it would, to all intents and purposes, *be* the original ditch. The earth that had washed into it could be peeled away from the sides easily with a

12

trowel. Indeed, it could simply have been shoveled out, just as the original builders had done, except that this earth would have to be examined carefully for artifacts. It was also necessary to be on the look-out for evidence of a palisade standing vertically along the bottom of the ditch—a common feature with structures such as a fort.

The "scarp" and "counterscarp" (the inner and outer slopes of the ditch) showed no erosion over the bottom 3 feet or so (the depth of the ditch averaged 5 feet below the 1585 ground level). This was attributable both to the character of the hard, dense subsoil and to the probability that some filling had occurred soon after the fort was built. But even the first filling from erosion took place after the colonists had left (in 1586), inasmuch as an Indian campfire was found at the bottom of the ditch. A second such campfire, found 2 feet higher, provides some clue as to how long the Indians remained in the vicinity. Indians seem to have been present to occupy this convenient windbreak at the first opportunity, but they found that the ditch offered better protection than the fort itself. Each of these hearths contained broken Indian pottery but no European objects, although (as will be explained below) any available fire-resistant material was utilized to support the Indians' pointed pots. Other evidence to suggest that this was an Indian village was lacking. More likely, it was a base used by Indians to tend their fields and protect their crops from animals or as a hunting outpost.

More cultural material than anticipated was found in the ditch fill. It included such unrelated items as an iron sickle lying on the very bottom, an iron auger, one of a set of nested brass balance weights, a chunk of pure smelted copper (similar to a specimen found under the parapet

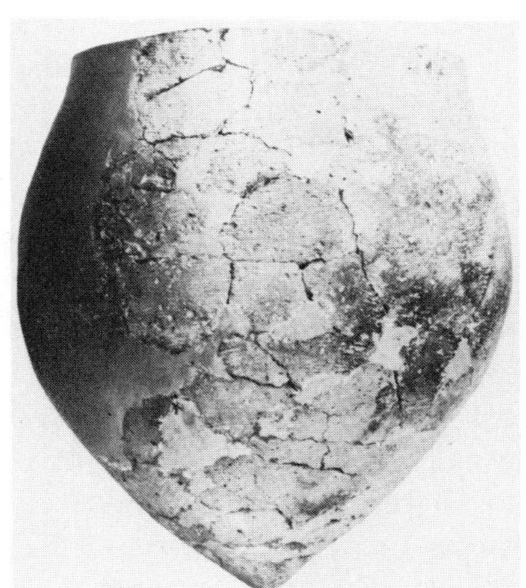

A typical clay Indian pot, with pointed base, making it necessary to support the vessel in a campfire by stacking fuel around it or using almost anything the Indians could get their hands on, such as old broken pots. The 130 sherds that were used in restoring this specimen were found near one of the campfires in the partially filled fort ditch. The overall height of this large pot was about 15 inches, while a nearly whole one found nearby was only half as large. From Harrington, *Search for the Cittie of Ralegh*, **Figure 33**.

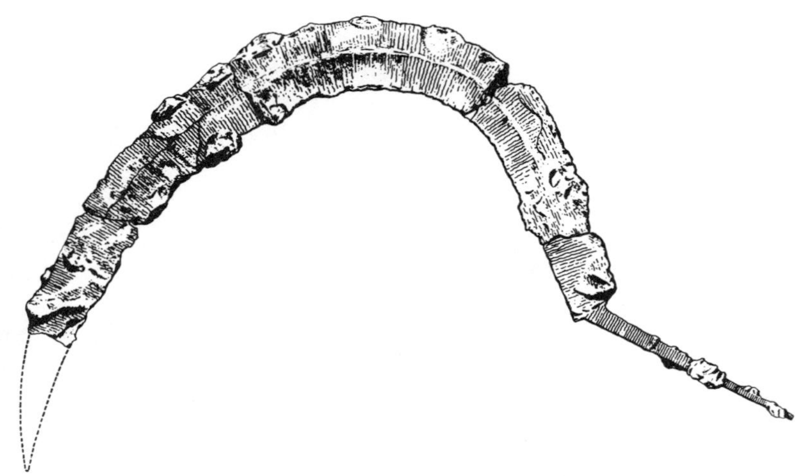

This wrought iron sickle originally measured some 22 inches along its curved blade, not including the tine for the wooden handle. Here was one of the useful items overlooked by the Indians, probably because it had been tramped into the very bottom of the fort ditch, where it was quickly covered with silt washed down from the parapet. This is one of the few artifacts found that reveals anything about the planned, or actual, activities of the colonists. From Harrington, *Search for the Cittie of Ralegh*, **Figure 14.**

remnant), several fragments of Spanish olive jars, a glass bead, and two sherds of Spanish majolica, possibly from an apothecary jar. More intriguing than any of this odd array was one brick fragment and one small piece of flat roofing tile, both found so deep in the fill that they could not possibly have worked their way down at a later time. The significance of these two fragments was not fully realized until later, when additional examples were found in a more revealing context. None of these objects revealed anything about the fort or threw much light on the possessions or activities of the colonists—either those stationed at the fort or those living in what was presumed to have been the nearby settlement.

In retrospect, rebuilding the fort still seems fully justified. The precise amount of earth necessary for reconstructing the parapet was known—namely, what came out of the ditch plus some compensation for the parade having been lowered and for the small amount of erosion that had taken place at the top of the ditch walls. The width of the parapet was known quite precisely from archaeological evidence, as discussed above. And descriptions of other earthworks of the period, as well as instructions in contemporary manuals (not to mention John White's fine drawing of a similar structure in Puerto Rico) are known to exist. Details such as gun platforms and embrasures would largely involve

14

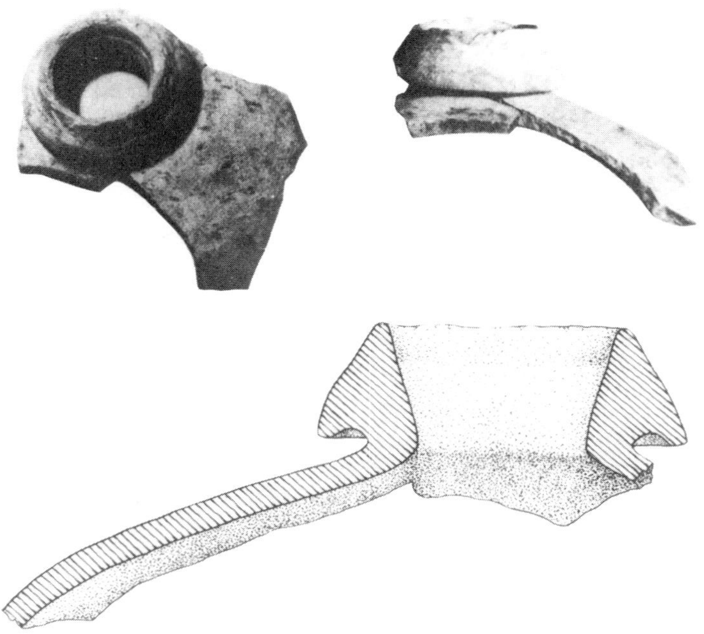

Several sherds of typical Spanish "olive jars" were found in the fort excavation, including this fragment from the very bottom of the fort ditch. These ceramic vessels, up to a foot in diameter (but usually smaller), were used for holding all sorts of liquids and may have served at the fort for storing water. Their presence at Fort Raleigh is a reminder of the contacts the colonists had with the Spanish in the Caribbean on their way to Roanoke Island. From Harrington, *Search for the Cittie of Ralegh*, **Figure 20**.

guesswork. This much conjecture seemed justified, and it was decided to proceed.

No serious thought was ever given to rebuilding such dubious features as structures within the fort or devices for protecting the two entrances. The major liberty taken in developing the site was in planting grass on the bare earth to prevent erosion. (It was impossible to face the problem of having the fort badly eroded by the first rainstorm, as seems to have occurred 400 years ago.) Ralph Lane would probably be surprised at the fort's pristine appearance, and his military sensibilities would doubtless be disturbed by the sight of the many large trees growing so close to the parapet—trees capable of shielding Indians or Spaniards from the eyes and musket balls of his garrison. Nevertheless, he would certainly recognize the reconstructed fort if he were to see it today.

III. The Elusive Settlement Site

History reveals, as the saying goes, that in the mid-summer of 1585 108 Englishmen were put ashore at some place near the north end of Roanoke Island and that these men started at once to build a fort and houses. Contemporary references to the colonists' place of residence include: "the place of our settlement or inhabitation," "our home Roanoke," "the towne," "place where we dwelt," and "the place which they inhabited." But history apparently is incapable of revealing what these houses looked like, except that they were thatched and had lofts or upper stories. It implies that the fort was separated from the houses but does not say whether by a few yards or a mile. It fails to indicate how these 108 officers, soldiers, craftsmen, laborers, and others were sheltered. There were no women or children in this first colony. Were there barracks or cottages? Was there a mess hall, a storehouse, a chapel? How many buildings were there? Were they clustered together, lined up along a street, or just tucked haphazardly among the trees? For that matter, were there any trees where the colonists placed their settlement, or did they take advantage of an area already cleared by the Indians for raising their crops? Dozens of related questions come to mind—for which no answers are even hinted at in the contemporary documents.

Things did not work out as anticipated by Sir Walter Ralegh and his backers; and when Sir Francis Drake arrived in June, 1586, the discouraged band soon decided to return with him to England and abandon the first English attempt to establish a colony in the New World. A few days after they departed, Richard Grenville arrived with reinforcements. Finding that the settlement had been abandoned, he left a small holding party of fifteen men to try to maintain what little had already been gained. Again, the records are not specific, but common sense compels the assumption that this group occupied some of the buildings that had just been vacated.

The following year, 1587, a second effort was made to plant a colony, bringing to Roanoke Island about 116 settlers—but this time including some women and children. The settlers could find no trace of the fifteen men left the year before—other than one skeleton, an eerie introduction to America! According to the records, they found the "forte was rased downe but all the houses standing unhurt," with the lower floors "overgrown with melons." The colonists set about at once to repair the houses and to build new "cottages" as needed. How many and what sort of houses—other than what the word "cottage" may imply—can only be guessed when it is borne in mind that this second contingent included families with children. The settlers of 1587 made no mention of repairing the "rased down" fort, possibly suggesting that they had other plans for sheltering themselves.

The Spanish kept England busy during the next few years, but when members of a relief expedition finally arrived at Roanoke Island in 1590, they found that the settlers had completely disappeared, having left the cryptic word "CROATOAN" carved on a tree or large post and the letters "CRO" on a tree near the shore. John White's detailed account of the 1590 voyage indicates that members of the relief expedition "found the houses taken downe, and the place very strongly enclosed with a high palisado of great trees, with cortynes and flankers very Fort-like."[8] This would suggest the presence of bastions and connecting curtain walls built of logs or heavy planks, consistent with plans for fortified enclosures of that period. Once again, except for mentioning the impressive "palisado," the historical record reveals absolutely nothing about the settlement, although it confirms the general location as being at the north end of the island.

All in all, the dozens of documents relating to the Ralegh effort to plant a colony in North America are distressingly silent on almost every important detail of interest to an archaeologist intent on excavating the site. All questions concerning the physical appearance of the settlement and the everyday life of the colonists have been left for archaeology to answer—a formidable and almost hopeless challenge in this instance. But even before attempting to answer these questions, archaeologists require a site on which to dig. Unlike the ruins of the fort, there were absolutely no surface indications that Europeans had ever been on Roanoke Island, let alone lived there, during the sixteenth century.

One reason why no surface evidence from the Ralegh settlement could be found (provided there was any there to be seen) is that windblown sand had spread over the entire area from a depth of 2 inches up to 10 or more feet, all of it having been deposited since the colonists abandoned the site. This condition was evident in the test trenches, with modern bottle caps being the prevalent artifacts in the sand layer; and only very occasionally was anything older found lying on the sixteenth-century, pre-sand surface—including occasional Indian potsherds. A welcome observation that also showed up in the test trenches was that the area of the 18.5-acre historic site had never been under cultivation. The large trees alone (some being an estimated 100 years old) attested to this; but the characteristic plow zone was absent, the upper layer just under the wildblown sand being natural forest humus grading into the yellow, sandy-clay subsoil. This condition would normally have been ideal for archaeology, but the relatively dense growth of trees over the entire site, as well as a paved road winding through the area, made effective archaeology difficult.

In spite of the physical problems, the lack of surface evidence, and the impreciseness of documentary evidence concerning the settlement's location, once the entrance to the fort was found, everyone was highly optimistic that some sort of evidence of the habitation area would be unearthed directly west of the fort. Therefore, this was where the search began—with high expectations. The plan that was followed was to dig continuous 5-foot-wide trenches to extend westward from the fort and to test as much of the area as feasible. Initially the sand layer and recent leaf mold that had developed on it were removed; then the floor of the trench was gone over with a magnetic metal detector in the hope of pinpointing any older metal objects. This operation yielded a few post-settlement nails and the like, plus a large number of bottle caps. Finally, the original topsoil was removed and the trench floor examined for intrusions.

Had it been known with certainty that the settlement site was in the presumed area, cutting a few trees might have been warranted; but destroying this prize asset could not be justified until something more definite was discovered. Therefore, the only recourse was to dodge in and out among the trees, attempting to do as little damage as possible but still exploring enough ground to be reasonably confident that evidence of former habitation (if it existed) would be encountered and recognized as such. It was impossible, of course, to test the ground under some of the higher dunes or the area occupied by the *Lost Colony* amphitheater.

What sort of archaeological evidence could one expect to find? The buildings would have been constructed largely of wood, all of which would have disappeared by 1947, when the test trenching began. Even if wattle-and-daub walls (clay plastered on woven laths or other natural material) had been used, evidence of such construction would be gone unless the buildings had burned and the clay had been hardened by heat. Or, if such construction had been used for chimneys—a common practice where stone or brick was not available—some evidence would probably remain. Disturbances of the subsoil from frame construction could be expected only if the timber frames of the buildings included heavy posts sunk into the ground. Such construction was frequently used a half century or more after the Ralegh colony was planted, as recent archaeology in Virginia and Maryland has shown.

No one expected, therefore, to find any structural remains at Fort Raleigh. But 108, then 15, and finally an even larger group of people cannot live in a concentrated settlement for three to five years without leaving considerable evidence scattered about. This fact has been demonstrated innumerable times at other archaeological sites. Tossing refuse out the kitchen door was a common practice, even in the best households. The most common trash heap would contain remains from the kitchen, such as animal and fish bones, clam- and oystershells, charred corncobs, and other types of garbage that would not disintegrate through the years; and, of course, there would be plenty of ashes from the fireplace. No one was expecting to find many broken dishes, since eating utensils would probably have been mostly of wood—although the colonists, particularly the 1587 group, certainly had some ceramic vessels. Even metal objects sometimes got broken and could not be mended, so portions of iron cooking utensils, possibly some cutlery, pothooks for the fireplace, and other household appurtenances could reasonably be anticipated.

When the colonists of 1587 left their homes on Roanoke Island— wherever they went or for whatever reason they departed—they almost certainly did not lug everything they owned along with them. Some things would have appealed to the Indians, who would have salvaged everything conceivably of use to them. But no Indian society was so dedicated to tidiness that its members would feel inclined to clean up the clamshells and other refuse left by the untidy English. It just made good sense, therefore, that if enough exploratory trenches were dug across the most likely location of the settlement site—that is, westward from the fort—some evidence of previous human occupation would show up.

But there was a second clue in the search for the settlement site: the "high palisado of great trees," with which members of the 1590 expedition were sufficiently impressed to record. In 1947, when the search for the town site began, it was generally assumed that such a feature would have consisted of logs standing in a trench and would have left clear-cut visible evidence in the smoothed floor of the trench. Since then, some new light has been thrown on how palisades might have been constructed around a settlement of that period. To build these palisades, planks were attached to stringers fastened to posts several feet apart. One wonders if such a feature would have been referred to as "a high palisado of great trees." But no matter how it was built, it is reasonably certain that there had been a continuous palisade around the settlement. Thus, one of the things it was hoped might be detected in the test trenches, in addition to the usual household refuse, was some evidence of a "high palisado."

The test trenching undertaken during the first season (1947) was confined to an area immediately west of the fort and outward from the newly discovered fort entrance. It was not too surprising or unduly discouraging not to have found much European material, since it was always assumed that there was some separation between the settlement and the fort. But even this unproductive excavating was not entirely in vain: a few sherds of Indian pottery, found lying directly on the old topsoil, provided the basis for a rough estimate as to when the sand was deposited.

During the second season (1948) a much larger area, consisting of most of the 18.5-acre historic site (except for the higher sand dunes and the *Lost Colony* facilities) was explored. This was followed in 1953 by limited testing to the west, where the Elizabethan Garden was being developed. In addition, a single long trench was dug east of the fort on private property. In all, over 4,000 lineal feet of test trenches, 5 feet wide, were excavated; but virtually no evidence—no more than a "handful" of nonaboriginal objects—was found to suggest that Europeans had lived there. One subsurface feature, a pit about 4 feet square and 4½ feet deep, the bottom half of which was filled with charcoal, was encountered in 1947. Was this possibly a pit in which charcoal was being made for use in a portable hand forge (which the records happen to mention as having been set up in Puerto Rico for making nails)? This is certainly stretching the imagination and shows how far an archaeologist will go to try to make something out of almost nothing. Most disappointing was the failure to find any trace whatever of the anticipated trench for supporting the logs of the putative palisade.

As had already been discovered at the fort excavation, Indians had been in the vicinity of this neighborhood before and after the colonists were there. Not surprisingly, most of the Indian pottery fragments from

20

the test trenches were found near the fort entrance, and always in the original topsoil beneath the sand. Obviously, the events that caused sand to be blown up from the shore and inland several hundred feet happened *after* the Indians had departed from this area and can have only an indirect bearing on the questions surrounding the location of the fort and settlement—although they may possibly have some relationship to the erosion that presumably has occurred along the north shore of Roanoke Island.

The archaeological evidence available in 1953 led to the conclusion that either the settlement was not located in the area tested or that not enough evidence was left to permit its identification through the testing method employed. Several approaches could be followed if the search were to continue: (1) The sand dunes could be removed (except where the *Lost Colony* facilities are involved) and the untested 100-yard strip back from the shore explored. (2) The trees from the most likely area west and southwest of the fort could be cut down, allowing more intensive and methodical excavations to be carried out. (3) The trench-testing procedure could be extended over a wider area—but where? And why? (4) Underwater exploration could be conducted along the shore near the historic site, where erosion is reputed to have cut back the shoreline (some say several hundred feet, but this is doubtful).

None of these alternatives was attractive or feasible, so the search was called off and a policy of marking time agreed upon. This meant keeping a close watch for some clue to turn up at any likely place that might be construed as being "toward the north end of the island." To this end, every effort has been made to keep both the residents of Roanoke Island and National Park Service personnel aware of the problem and cooperative in reporting anything relevant that might be found on their property. It is asking a great deal, however, to expect that even the most conscientious citizen would report a suspicious find, in light of the specter of his or her well-tended lawn being dug up by an archaeological crew.*

Over and over the question was asked: "Why couldn't John White have shown the settlement and fort on one of his maps and saved all this uncertainty and agonizing effort to read something more definitive into the contemporary documents?" Perhaps he did, and historians simply are not properly interpreting the evidence. Or perhaps there may

---

Editor's note: Nevertheless, several local people are reported to have found significant or potentially significant artifacts but have been unable to arouse the interest of the National Park Service or any other agency.

actually have been such a priceless document among White's drawings, which he buried for safekeeping but which the Indians were reported to have discovered and destroyed. In any event, after several years of fruitless investigation, archaeologists were no further ahead on locating and excavating the settlement site— although they were reasonably sure as to where the site was *not* located.

IV. A Fortuitous Discovery

Not until 1959 did the policy of watchful waiting bear fruit in the form of an accidental discovery of a mysterious archaeological feature later identified as a type of sunken structure; ironically, this "fortuitous discovery" was literally underfoot. And, most unexpectedly, it lay only a few feet from the fort, directly below the paved entrance driveway, which had been walked and driven over for years. It was as pure a piece of luck as one would ever experience at an archaeological site. Providentially, the find that had been stumbled on at Fort Raleigh was recognized as of possible importance and immediately reported to a responsible—and responsive—person. Subsequent excavation of the feature showed quite convincingly that luck plays an important role in archaeology and that no clues—especially those bearing on the precise location of the settlement site at Fort Raleigh—should be dismissed without being looked into.

The intriguing story of the discovery and excavation of this strange feature began in 1959 with the digging of a narrow trench to carry utility lines to the restored fort. At one point where this trench crossed the paved road near the fort, a small area containing ashes, fire-hardened clay, and what appeared to be underfired brick fragments was encountered at a depth of some 18 inches below the pavement. Someone on the crew realized that this was something that would not be found naturally at this depth, so it was recorded and the utility line moved a safe distance away. (Fortunately, it was moved in the right direction!) Some samples of the clay and brick fragments were retrieved for examination by "specialists," and the trench was backfilled and left for archaeological examination at some future date.

Not until six years later did an archaeologist actually get around to looking into this discovery. This delay reflected the view that probably nothing significant would be found—at least nothing to justify the inconvenience of closing the main road into the *Lost Colony* amphitheater and the restored fort. After all, what would one expect to find at this location less than 30 feet from the fort? There, under the paved road, was what appeared to be just another Indian hearth such as those found

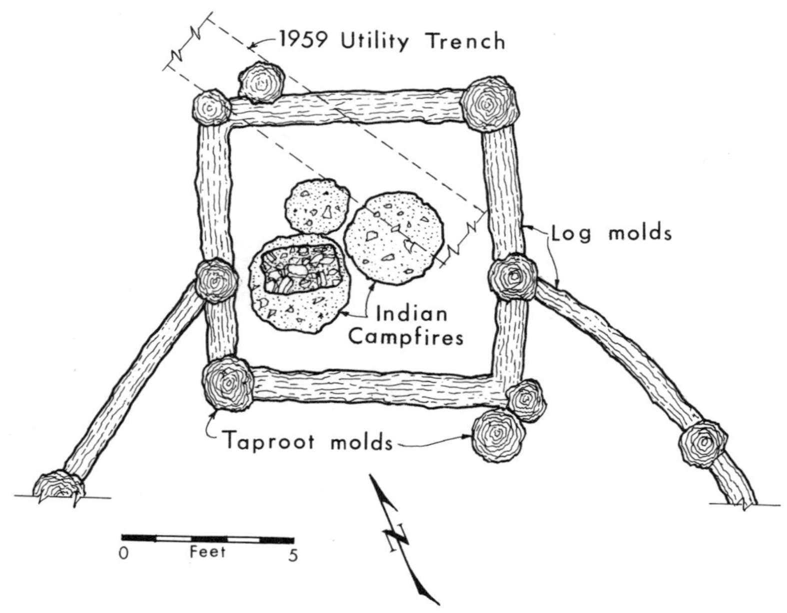

Plan of outwork, showing sunken square bounded by horizontal log molds and traces of logs extending out from two sides of the square. Apparently the logs were wedged between trees or stumps, or else trees grew out of the original posts. The feature was discovered quite by accident when a utility trench was dug in 1959. It has not yet been identified, although it must have served some defensive function. Further excavation in this area might possibly provide the answer—and might even lead to the location of the settlement site. Drawing supplied by the author.

in the partially filled fort ditch. But both curiosity and a sense of professional obligation overcame the initial reluctance to look into this find.

The first feature to be uncovered in what was expected to be a two- or three-day excavation (and the original find in the utility trench) was, indeed, the remnant of a small, circular campfire identical to those found previously at the fort. Using the fort ditch as a shelter from the wind made sense, but what was an Indian campfire doing out in the open? There had to be some practical explanation (practical to an Indian, at least). And so the investigation was launched; eventually, it covered an irregular area of some 40 feet at its maximum width.

In addition to the campfire found in the utility trench, two more turned up nearby, forming a cluster of three circular features of varying size. One of the three was quite impressive, with a pile of nearly three dozen bricks, whole or broken, lying in a sunken rectangular depression in the center of the hearth. In this same feature were sherds from Indian pottery and pieces from a broken ceramic bottle ("costrel") of European manufacture. Even more surprising, the hearth also con-

24

tained several fragments of flat roofing tiles. Beyond any doubt, all of this nonaboriginal material had been brought to this spot from the fort or the settlement (most likely, of course, from the adjacent fort) for the express purpose of steadying the unwieldy pointed-based Indian pots. And, just as clearly, it had been brought there after the settlement had been abandoned.

Although the chronological history of this group of features ended with the Indians, the archaeological story involving the English colonists only begins there. As usually happens in archaeology, the historical sequence is inverted, or reversed. As the excavation was extended beyond (out from) the three Indian hearths, dark streaks were noted on the floor of the trench. Examination revealed that the streaks formed a rough square from 7 to 8 feet across on the inside. Vertical sections through the streaks showed them to be circular, each almost a foot in diameter—obviously the remnants of logs. All that remained was stained earth—earth only a little darker than the adjacent group but sufficiently visible in photographs. Each of these horizontal logs ended at an irregular, circular disturbance slightly larger than the logs. When first encountered, the disturbance resembled remains of huge posts, and the contemporary account of finding a "palisado of great trees" immediately came to mind. But further checking proved these roughly circular intrusions to be taproots of trees. The intrusions decreased in size as they went down, one being as deep as 5½ feet. Obviously, no implement capable of digging holes of this shape and depth existed in the late sixteenth century! The remains described here were too near the surface—where there had been considerable disturbance through the years—to indicate exactly what happened above the first, and lowest, of the logs; but it appeared that there were other logs above the first layer— at least on the three outer sides.

A shallow ditch was found outside the sunken square, the bottom being nearly 2 feet below the historic ground level. Lying on the very bottom of this ditch were a few fragments of a ceramic bottle; sherds of this very same bottle had been found in one of the campfires in the sunken area. Indeed, enough pieces were recovered from the two locations to enable the vessel to be restored to its original shape. A few Indian potsherds also were found at the bottom of the ditch—the same type of pottery as that found at the campfires. Clearly, Indians had taken advantage of the sunken structure as a sheltered spot for their campfires immediately after it had been vacated by the colonists. The Indians' use of the structure is extremely interesting, but it reveals nothing about

Part of a ceramic bottle ("costrel") partially restored from some twenty-five fragments found mostly in and near the campfires in the outwork. Several sherds of the same vessel were found at the bottom of the shallow ditch surrounding the structure, showing that the Indians made use of the outwork as soon as it was abandoned by the colonists—before the ditch started filling up from erosion. Such bottles had coverings of wickerwork to facilitate storing and carrying and were used as containers for various liquids such as oil, wine, or water. From Jean Carl Harrington, *An Outwork at Fort Raleigh: Further Archeological Excavations at Fort Raleigh National Historic Site, North Carolina* (Philadelphia: Eastern National Park and Monument Association, 1966), Figure 7.

when the feature was built, whether it constitutes a useful clue to the location of the settlement, or, for that matter, what it was.

As the exploration continued, it became obvious that this strange structure was not some isolated feature. Stains from horizontal logs on the floor of the excavation continued outward from the sunken square from midway along two of its three sides. Unlike the square, however, the ground between these extending arms was at the original ground level, not sunken. The hardest thing to explain was the absence of non-Indian artifacts (other than the bricks and tile fragments in the campfires and the fragments of the ceramic bottle). If the Indians were so enthralled by the Englishmen's refuse, why did they disdain the bottle?

What, then, was the purpose of this strange structure? And what, if anything, does it reveal about the Ralegh settlement? It most certainly was not of Indian origin, and it clearly dates from a period before the native population had left the immediate vicinity. The form of the structure, apparently a log-revetted breastwork with depressed floor, suggests a defensive function; and the approximate height of the apparent breastwork is dictated by the amount of earth thrown out of the small ditches and the degree to which the floor of the log-lined square was lowered.

The most plausible interpretation is that it was a special feature at one corner of the palisaded enclosure erected, so the record implies, by the second colonizing group. If so, it may well lead archaeologists directly to the settlement site, although, at this point, it is hard to reconcile the remains in question with the "high palisado of great trees." It is difficult to rationalize it as part of the 1585 earthwork, and even harder to regard it as a unit independent of either the fort or the settlement enclosure. For convenience, it has been called an "outwork," purposely a rather generalized term, although the more specific term "watchtower" has been proposed. For the present, the safest approach is simply to concede that it is both intriguing and inexplicable and that additional archaeology offers the only possible means to effect its identification. Merely speculating on it is frustrating and unproductive.

Once again, the search for the settlement site had to be suspended in spite of the possibility of rewards in continuing to work in this area of the "fortuitous discovery." Programmed development took precedence over archaeology, and no one could afford to rush in with a "salvage" project. It could keep; so once again, something was left for some archaeologist of the future.

V. Fort Raleigh Bricks: A True Story

Archaeologists are inclined to record detailed measurements of any bricks they happen to find in a dig and then draw conclusions—often unwarranted—from them. This "story" starts with the bricks from the Indian campfires in the mysterious "outwork" described above. It was obvious what the Indians used them for and that they must have been found nearby. As usual, the size of the bricks reveals very little, primarily because there were too few whole bricks to secure meaningful statistical measurements. Besides, the approximate date of the site was already known—at least to a more accurate degree than brick measurements could disclose.

What, then, could these bricks possibly reveal? A deep interest in them apparently originated in a contemporary bit of historical information purported to be a deposition made by a former member of the first Roanoke colony. The key portion of the purported deposition reads as follows: "as soon as they had disembarked, they began to make brick and tiles for a fort and houses." It has been difficult not to appear skeptical about this bit of documented history. The man responsible for giving this information to the Spanish at St. Augustine fifteen years after the alleged event signed his deposition "David Glavin, Irish soldier." It is possible that Glavin was merely attempting to impress the Spanish with the advanced state of the English colonization. But no matter; the point is that prior to the archaeological findings at Fort Raleigh, there was considerable doubt as to whether any credence should be given to this seemingly outlandish claim. No one, of course, dismisses such straight-forward documentary evidence out of hand. But even when the first brickbat was found deep in the fill of the fort ditch, explanations of how it might have gotten there were bandied about; one such explanation was the old archaeological standby that it had fallen down a gopher hole. No one then had the audacity to suggest that it might tie in with Glavin's deposition.

But with the discovery of all the bricks and a few roofing-tile fragments in the Indian campfires, one had to admit that the colonists did, in fact, have bricks and tiles that were either made on Roanoke Island or

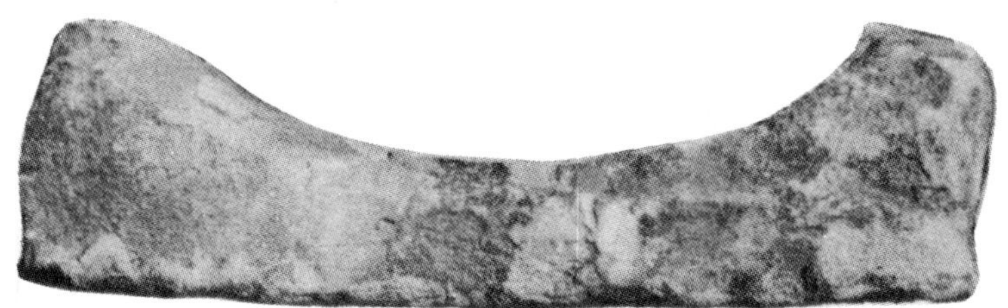

More than thirty whole bricks or portions of bricks were found in the three Indian campfires that had been dug into the sunken floor of the outwork. Most of these bricks had been abraded down to various shapes and sizes, probably through use as polishers and sharpeners of armor and weapons. The one shown above was most likely used for sharpening swords, pikes, or halberds. The Indians presumably found these bricks at the adjacent fort and made good use of them as pot supporters in their hearths. Laboratory tests reveal that these bricks were actually made at the new settlement, just as historical records claim. From Harrington, *An Outwork at Fort Raleigh*, Figure 8.

brought from England. There was no way to determine by size or general appearance what the source of these products was, so it was necessary to turn to a specialist in clay products. Samples of bricks and tiles as well as earth from several sources in the general vicinity of the site were sent to the laboratory of the United States Geological Survey for laboratory tests—with startling and thoroughly convincing results. The detailed report from the laboratory revealed that physically and chemically the bricks and local earth were identical in every respect—much too similar to be accounted for by simple coincidence. Most telling of all, the native earth contains a very small amount of the relatively rare mineral illite— in the identical proportion as in the brick samples. This chemical is destroyed at just under 1,600 degrees F., but it was still in the bricks in the correct proportion. Therefore, the bricks must have been fired at a relatively low temperature—at least 400 degrees lower than that required for producing first-class bricks. But even when some of the Fort Raleigh brick samples were fired at a much higher temperature, the quality of the product did not improve. The conclusion to be drawn from the examination of the brick samples is clear: the colonists did, indeed, attempt to make bricks but must have quickly discovered that the local earth was not at all suitable. Undoubtedly, they discovered this on the very first kiln load, for only experienced brickmakers would have embarked on such a project. But these first bricks—too soft and crumbly for construction purposes—were not wasted, as will be shown.

What about the tiles? If David Glavin was telling the truth about making bricks, can his word not also be taken concerning the tiles? The laboratory tests told quite a different story. The tile fragments from the excavations were well made (not warped, as some often were) and showed a physical and chemical composition entirely different from that of the bricks and local earth. On the present evidence, therefore, it must be concluded that the tiles represented by the few fragments found in the excavation were brought from England. Of course, David Glavin may not have been telling a tall story. The colonists could have intended to make both bricks and tiles but very quickly have given up on the tiles when they realized that the ingredients simply were not suitable. And, of course, they might have made some tiles that have not as yet shown up in the excavating.

As historically exciting and revealing as all this is, the brick story has barely begun. Most of the bricks found in the campfires were not ordinary bricks—although they had been at one time. Altogether, four whole bricks were found, plus enough fragments to account for several more. An entire chapter could be written on the probable process of making these bricks, but it has no bearing on the problem at hand. Far more important, and much more interesting, are the twenty specimens that had been ground to an amazing array of shapes and sizes—from little cubes to nearly whole bricks with one flat surface abraded to a uniform concave shape.

The only plausible explanation yet offered is that the relatively soft, lightly fired bricks, with their uniform abrasive surfaces, would have made ideal implements for polishing and sharpening iron objects, especially armor and weapons. Thus, the brickmaking venture apparently was not a completely wasted effort, although it did not enable the colonists to build better houses. And what a boon to the Indians to find this stock of supports for their cooking pots in the abandoned fort only a few yards away!

Like so much of the archaeological and documentary evidence pertaining to Fort Raleigh, the rather unconventional story of the bricks found in the Indian campfires raises all kinds of questions. If the earthen fort was not repaired by the second expedition (a conclusion based solely upon circumstantial evidence), the bricks must have been taken to the fort by the soldiers garrisoned there between 1585 and 1586. Then, according to this timetable, after the bricks had been used for less than a year, they simply lay there in the semiruined fort until they were salvaged by the Indians. Precisely what date this took place depends upon when the outwork was built and abandoned. (This is the kind of dilemma that archaeologists frequently face. The dates that these bricks were moved from one spot to another is really not too significant.)

More important is where the Indians found the bricks in the first place. None of the whole bricks had any signs of mortar on their surfaces, so it is likely that they were never moved from the kiln, let alone built into a foundation or chimney, until some enterprising soldier recognized their possibilities as sharpeners or polishers. The Indians then saw a different use for them, and once again they served a new and quite unanticipated function.[9]

VI. Fort Raleigh Archaeology: Retrospect and Prospect

Archaeological excavations at Fort Raleigh have produced considerable information. When analyzed in conjunction with documentary evidence, they reveal a great deal more than was known when digging was begun there by the National Park Service in 1947. Even so, archaeology has produced nothing that calls for any change in the script for Paul Green's drama—although a new look by David Quinn at the documentary evidence suggests that the second colonizing group possibly moved north to the Chesapeake Bay region rather than southward, as the cryptic message on the post or tree trunk seemed to imply. It is true that through archaeology the fort ruins have come to life, but in doing so they may have lost some of their romantic appeal as indistinct ruins. The fate of the "Lost Colony" is still a mystery, and the settlement site is still as elusive as ever.

Of the two primary objectives of archaeology at Fort Raleigh—locating (and possibly excavating) the settlement area and excavating and restoring the fort—only the second was achieved. Unlike the fort, however, test trenches in the area assumed to have been inhabited revealed in no uncertain terms that archaeologists were looking in the wrong place. On the other hand, the subsequent discovery of the outwork has stirred optimism that the houses might still be found—right where they had been assumed to be all along.

The fort project was, on the whole, a complete success. Adequate evidence was at hand to permit the restoration of the fort ditch and the parapet, although there was found no reliable information concerning what sort of structures stood within the fort. Nor was there gained any insight into what the members of the garrison did in their spare time, other than polish their armor with underfired bricks. Removal of the earth from the fort ditch showed that it had filled up relatively slowly. Thus, the contemporary statement that the fort had been "rased down" may not mean that it was demolished in one fell swoop. But the physical remains do seem to support the documentary evidence that the "rased down" fort was not rebuilt in 1587. Apparently, the second group of colonists had other ideas for defending themselves; perhaps they had

32

begun to worry more about the natives than about the Spanish.

When the search for the settlement site is renewed, as it surely will be one day, it will almost certainly employ different approaches than those used some forty years ago. There have been developed within the past dozen or so years new techniques capable of locating and defining cultural remains without the necessity of putting a shovel in the ground. But even these sophisticated methods will be handicapped by the heavy vegetation at the site and the thick sand deposits. If this type of survey is deemed practical, it would probably be used before any further excavating is done. But no matter what it reveals, there is bound to be an insistent clamor to follow up the features associated with the outwork. No one can offer a completely acceptable explanation for these remains, other than their having been part of the 1587 "palisado." In fact, Phillip Evans of the Fort Raleigh staff has pointed out the similiarity in plan of these features with those recently uncovered at Martin's Hundred in Virginia, which quite clearly are the remains of a palisaded enclosure dating from 1619. The picture, then, is not quite so gloomy as it seemed in 1953, but ambiguous contemporary documents subject to conflicting interpretation by different scholars must still be contended with.

In 1947, when still confident of finding the settlement site not far from the fort, archaeologists were quite content to declare unequivocally that the traditional fort ruins were those of Ralph Lane's "new fort in Virginia." But failure to find positive evidence of the settlement has raised some doubts, and alternative locations have been proposed—both for the fort and the settlement. These are based solely on interpretation of the documentary evidence and the argument that the little earthwork at Fort Raleigh is too small to be Lane's primary fort. Obviously, the burden of proof lies with anyone disputing the identity of the traditional site, but it is useful to have questions raised on almost any subject relating to Fort Raleigh.

The attempt to solve the enigma of Fort Raleigh will undoubtedly continue until the matter is settled once and for all through archaeology. Beyond further exploration at the outwork, it is impossible to discern at this point precisely where that archaeology will take place. If additional documentary evidence (from Spanish archives, for example) should turn up, or some chance find be made of cultural material of the right period, it would certainly not be ignored, no matter what the prevailing theories and conclusions might be. And someday, evidence of David Glavin's brickyard, which must have left a treasure trove of archaeological evidence, may be stumbled upon. Even if nothing materializes from extension of the outwork excavation or remote sensing, it is hard to imagine that all the evidence normally left at a site such as Fort Raleigh will go undetected forever. For the time being, however, it will simply have to be admitted that the "Lost Colony" is still lost—though perhaps not quite so lost as it was fifty years ago—and that the enigma of Fort Raleigh is still very much alive.

Notes

[1] Phillip W. Evans, "Justification for Further Archeological Exploration for the Settlement Site at Fort Raleigh National Historic Site" (unpublished report, July, 1981, on file at Fort Raleigh National Historic Site, Roanoke Island).

[2] David Beers Quinn (ed.), *The Roanoke Voyages, 1584-1590* (London: Hakluyt Society, 2 volumes, 1955), hereinafter cited as Quinn, *The Roanoke Voyages*, is the primary source.

[3] John Lawson, *A New Voyage to Carolina*, edited by Hugh Talmage Lefler (Chapel Hill: University of North Carolina Press, 1967), 62.

[4] A glacis is an artificial buildup of earth at the top of an outer ditch slope, which tapers away from a fort; it was used to prevent attackers from lying flat on the ground and thus positioning themselves below the line of fire from the fort.

[5] Examples of methods used by archaeologists in establishing relative dates of intrusive features are (1) cutting an intrusion into another of a known date; and (2) determining the age of objects found within a feature.

[6] An interesting sidelight is that an identical specimen was found at an Indian site near Cape Hatteras in 1938, but not too much significance should be read into this intriguing happenstance. It certainly should not be cited as evidence that the colonists went south when they left Roanoke Island, tempting as this interpretation might be.

[7] This is but one example of the difficulty inherent in reading anything significant into the scanty and unrelated artifacts recovered at the Fort Raleigh dig. Ordinarily an archaeologist finds literally bushels of discarded objects and refuse that, taken as a whole, can be used effectively in interpreting what transpired at a site—but not so at Fort Raleigh.

[8] Quinn, *The Roanoke Voyages*, II, 614.

[9] If the 1959 utility trench had been dug even a foot farther to the east, this exciting sequence of events would not have come to light.

Additional Reading

Durant, David N. *Ralegh's Lost Colony*. New York: Atheneum, 1981. A recent and readable account, making extensive use of the documents and new findings. Some of the interpretations are controversial.

Harrington, Jean Carl. *Search for the Cittie of Ralegh: Archaeological Excavations at Fort Raleigh National Historic Site, North Carolina.* Archaeological Research Series, No. 6. Washington: National Park Service, United States Department of the Interior, 1962. A detailed report on the 1948-1953 excavation and restoration of the fort and exploratory trenching in the surrounding area.

_______________ . *An Outwork at Fort Raleigh: Further Archeological Excavations at Fort Raleigh National Historic Site, North Carolina.* Philadelphia: Eastern National Park and Monument Association, 1966. A detailed report on the excavation of the feature discovered in 1959, which may be part of the "palisado."

Porter, Charles W., III. *Adventures to a New World*. Washington: National Park Service, United States Department of the Interior, 1972. A summary of the historical and archaeological evidence, with reproductions of twelve of the John White paintings.

_______________ . "Fort Raleigh National Historic Site, North Carolina: Part of the Settlement Sites of Sir Walter Raleigh's Colonies of 1585-1586 and 1587." *North Carolina Historical Review*, XX (January, 1943), 22-42.

Quinn, David Beers. *The Roanoke Voyages, 1584-1590*. London: Hakluyt Society, 1955. A definitive study of the documents relating to the site by the preeminent authority on the subject. The volume contains a summary and discussion of archaeological findings through 1948.

Quinn, David B., and Alison M. Quinn, eds. *The First Colonists: Documents on the Planting of the First English Settlements in North America, 1584-1590.* Raleigh: Division of Archives and History, North Carolina Department of Cultural Resources, 1982.